My Book About Toys

Toys play an important part in the lives of children everywhere. This book aims to help young readers describe and explain the different kinds of toys they play with – toys for indoors or outdoors, for playing with on their own or with friends, for building up or knocking down, simple toys or complicated toys, bought or home-made. The book goes on to look at toys from different parts of the world, and from the past.

My Book About

The Body	Houses and Homes
Clothes	Toys
Food	Weather

Editor: Anna Girling
Designer: Loraine Hayes

First published in 1991 by
Wayland (Publishers) Ltd
61 Western Road, Hove
East Sussex BN3 1JD, England

British Library Cataloguing in Publication Data
Jackman, Wayne
Toys.
1. Toys
I. Title   II. Series
688.72

ISBN 0 7502 0120 7

Typeset by Kalligraphic Design Ltd, Horley, Surrey
Printed and bound by Casterman S.A., Belgium

Words that are **underlined** in the text
are explained in the glossary on page 22.

My Book About

Toys

WAYNE JACKMAN

Look at this toy shop.

Do you have any toys like these?
Perhaps you have got a teddy bear.

This boy likes toy cars and lorries.

He is using a **remote control**.
The lorry is his **favourite** toy.

This girl is doing a **jigsaw puzzle**.
Jigsaw puzzles are fun to do when you are on your own.

What toys do you play with when you are on your own?

These children are friends.
They are playing together with a toy tea set.

Do you play with toys with your friends?

Some toys are fun to play with indoors.
You can play with them even when it is raining outside.

What is your favourite toy for indoors?

These children are playing outside in a big sand-pit. They are using buckets and spades.

Let's count the buckets in the picture.

Here are some toy bricks.

These children are building a tower out of bricks.
Watch out! It might fall down!

Some toys are meant to be knocked down.

This girl is playing a game of **skittles**.
She has knocked down one skittle.
What colour is it?

Some toys are very **simple**.
All you need for skipping is a piece of rope.

These children are skipping in the playground.
You can skip by yourself or you can skip with some
of your friends.

This toy looks **complicated**.
There are lots of tiny pieces.

The boy is painting some of the pieces.
Can you guess what he is making?

You can make toys yourself. This boy has made a paper **aeroplane**.

Do you think it will fly well?

Can you make a boat out of a plastic pot?

It will **float** well in a pool of water.
This pool of water is in a dustbin lid.

These children in Africa have made tiny cars.

They use the sticks to pull the cars along. They have lined up for a race.

Have you got a toy <u>whistle</u>?

This boy from India is blowing a whistle.
He has made himself some sun-glasses. Very smart!

These toys are very old.
They are all made of wood.

Do you have any toys that your Mum or Dad once played with?

Be careful not to break them.

Children have liked **rocking horses** for hundreds of years.

These are new rocking horses. They look very real.
Would you like to sit on one of them?

This room looks a mess.
There are toys everywhere.

Does your room look like this sometimes?
Perhaps a grown-up tells you to tidy it up.

This looks much tidier.

The boys have put all the toys neatly away in the proper places.

Glossary

Aeroplane A machine that flies through the air.

Complicated Made up of lots of different parts.

Favourite The thing you like the most.

Float To stay at the top of water, without sinking to the bottom.

Jigsaw puzzle A toy with lots of pieces that you fit together to make a picture.

Remote control A machine that you can use to make a toy move, even when you are far away from it.

Rocking horses Toy horses that children can sit on.

Simple Not difficult or complicated.

Skittles A game in which you throw a ball at some pieces of wood or plastic, shaped like bottles, and try to make them fall over.

Whistle A tube with holes in it that you blow through to make a noise.

Picture acknowledgements

The publishers would like to thank the following for providing the photographs for this book: Eye Ubiquitous 4 (Paul Seheult), 11 (Roger Chester), 15 (Dave Fobister), 20, 21; Lesley Howling 12; John and Penny Hubley 17; Hutchison Library 16 (Anna Tully); Nick Nicholson 18; Topham Picture Library 19; Wayland Picture Library cover (Zul Mukhida), 8 (Trevor Hill); Timothy Woodcock 5, 6, 7, 9, 10, 13, 14.

Books to read

The Know How Book of Action Toys by Heather Amery (Usborne, 1989)
Marbles, Hopscotch and Jacks by John Dinneen (Angus & Robertson, 1987)

More Tricks and Games with Paper by Paul Jackson (Angus & Robertson, 1988)
Party Games and Rotten Tricks by John Dinneen (Angus & Robertson, 1986)

Places to visit

Great Britain
Bethnal Green Museum of Childhood,
Cambridge Heath Road,
London E2 9PA.

London Toy and Model Museum,
Lancaster Gate,
London.

Museum of Childhood,
42 High Street,
Edinburgh.

Museum of Childhood,
Sudbury Hall,
Sudbury,
Derbyshire DE6 5HT.

Pollock's Toy Museum,
1 Scala Street,
London W1P 1LT.

Other toy museums are listed in *Museums and Galleries in Great Britain and Ireland* (British Leisure Publications) at your library.

Australia
The Children's Museum,
Museum of Victoria,
328 Swanston Street,
Melbourne VIC 3000.

Canada
The Puppet Centre,
171 Avondale Avenue,
North York,
Toronto M2N 2V4.

Index